Famous Forts Throughout American History

Fort Ticonderoga

Charles W. Maynard

The Rosen Publishing Group's
PowerKids Press™
New York

To Janice, my friend, wife, and favorite writer

Published in 2002 by The Rosen Publishing Group, Inc.
29 East 21st Street, New York, NY 10010

First Edition

Book Design: Michael Caroleo

Project Editor: Kathy Campbell

Photo Credits: pp. 4 (map), 7, 11 © North Wind Pictures; pp. 4 (Champlain), 20 © CORBIS; p. 8 photograph by Daniel R. Caroleo; p. 12 © Mark Gibson/CORBIS; p. 15 © David Muench/CORBIS; p. 16 © Archive Photos; p. 19 © Michael Phillip Manheim/International Stock; p. 19 (framed flag) © Fort Ticonderoga Museum.

Gift 8/04

Maynard, Charles W. (Charles William), 1955—
    Fort Ticonderoga / Charles W. Maynard.— 1st ed.
        p. cm. — (Famous forts throughout American history)
Includes index.
    ISBN 0-8239-5836-1 (library binding: alk. paper)
    1. Fort Ticonderoga (N.Y.) —History—Juvenile literature. 2. Ticonderoga (N.Y.) —History—French and Indian War, 1755–1763—Juvenile literature. 3. Ticonderoga (N.Y.) —History—Revolution, 1775–1783—Juvenile literature.
[1. Fort Ticonderoga (N.Y.)] I. Title. II. Series.
    E199 .M475 2002
Curr   974.7'53—dc21
                                                            00-011416

Manufactured in the United States of America

Contents

Left: In 1609, the French explorer Samuel de Champlain visited the lake area that now bears his name. He and Algonquin warriors fought a band of Iroquois on land that later would become Fort Ticonderoga.

PLAN
OF THE FORT
at
TIENDEROGA,
at
the HEAD of
Lake Champlain;
1759.

A. *The Fort* .... I. *9 Ovens*
B. *Stone work* ..... K. *Brick Kiln*
C. *Earth work* ..... L. *Lime Kilns*
D. *Wharf* .... M. *Old French Batt.*
E. *Store house for* N. *The French Lines*
   the Naval Stores O. *Batterys thereon*
F. *The Redoubt* ... P. *Abbatti of branches*
G. *Lower Battery*   *of Trees before ẙ Lines*
   for 2 Guns ..... a. *Wharf & Harbour for*
H. *Store houses*   *ẙ Vessels of War stockaded*
   for Provisions. *round to prevent the Ene-*
                      my destroying them.

Scale 400 Feet to an Inch.

Cheonderoga

In the state of New York, where the waters of Lake George flow through the La Chute River to empty into Lake Champlain, there is a point of land. The Iroquois called this **peninsula** Cheonderoga, which means "a place between two waters." To the Iroquois, Huron, and Abenaki peoples, Cheonderoga was at the crossroads of the Hudson River and Lake Champlain waterways. The rivers and lakes of New York were called The Great War Path because Native Americans traveled them for thousands of years in canoes to fight with one another.

Samuel de Champlain, a French **explorer**, visited the area with Huron warriors in 1609. They fought a band of Iroquois near where Fort Ticonderoga now stands.

A map of Fort Ticonderoga from 1759 shows the fort's important location at the point on a peninsula that the Iroquois called Cheonderoga. The fort controlled the key waterway, where Lake Champlain connects Lake George, for transportation and trading in the region.

The French Build a Fort

In the early 1700s, France and Great Britain both claimed the area in New York between French Canada (New France) and the British colonies on the East Coast. The two countries with their Native American **allies** fought over the land. The French began to build a fort at Cheonderoga in 1755 to guard The Great War Path. They started in the fall by cutting trees to clear the land on the point between Lake George and Lake Champlain. In the spring of 1756, they built strong walls of timber from the forest. The soldiers then dug ditches around the 7-foot- (2-m-) high walls, and piled the dirt against these walls. Three stone **barracks** were constructed to house the soldiers. The French soldiers called their new home Fort Carillon

This picture of Cheonderoga shows the frame of the fort in its early days. Engineer Michel Chartier drew the first fort's plans and wanted to name it Fort Vaudreuil. The French soldiers decided to call it Fort Carillon instead.

after a fur trader
named Philippe de
Carrion. Carrion had served
with French troops in New France in the
1660s. About 10 years later, Carrion
built a fur trading post at Cheonderoga. Later
the British would give Fort Carillon a new
name, Fort Ticonderoga.

Fort Ticonderoga

In winter the fort could safely hold 400 soldiers within its walls, although most battles were fought in the warm months of the year. In the summer, about 2,500 soldiers served at the fort. Tents outside the fort's walls, protected by more ditches, housed the extra men. At the entrance to the fort stand two 13-inch (33-cm) mortars, which are very short cannons used to shoot shells that explode.

The Structure of the Fort

During 1756–57, the French soldiers built a double-walled wooden fort. The space between the walls was filled with dirt for added protection against cannonballs. Later the wooden walls were covered with stone to slow the rotting of the wood. The shape of the fort was a large square with points, called **bastions**, at each corner. The stone barracks formed three sides, with a stone wall completing the square. Each bastion served a special purpose. One contained a **cistern** to collect and store water, another had ovens to bake bread, and a third had a **powder magazine** to store the gunpowder and **ammunition**. The fourth bastion held food and supplies. The soldiers gathered to parade and drill in the center of the fort, which was called the Place of Arms. Ditches with a step surrounded the fort so the soldiers could stand and shoot at the enemy. Trees and brush, called **abatis**, were stacked around the ditches to slow the attacking British soldiers.

The Fort Under Attack

From 1754 to 1763, Great Britain and France fought a war in North America. It was called the French and Indian War because the British colonists and their Native American friends fought the French and their Native American friends. The British attacked Fort Carillon on July 8, 1758, with more than 15,000 men. The French army at the fort numbered nearly 4,000. The French general, the Marquis de Montcalm, moved his soldiers to a hill, called the Heights of Carillon, near the fort and ordered ditches to be dug. The French soldiers stood in the ditches for protection as they fired at the British. Montcalm's soldiers fought hard and defeated the larger British army. In the following year, British general Jeffery Amherst circled the fort with soldiers and **artillery** so no supplies could get to the French. One night in July, the French blew up the powder magazine,

It took the British four days of heavy fighting to seize the fort. British general Jeffery Amherst captured the French fort on July 27, 1759. The French general, the Marquis de Montcalm, had part of the fort blown up as the French soldiers escaped to the north.

burned the fort, and then left it. The British repaired the fort and called it Fort Ticonderoga, a name similar to the Iroquois name, Cheonderoga.

The south barracks housed soldiers at Fort Ticonderoga. The troops at the fort used the howitzers, or short cannons, seen here to fire on attacking soldiers.

Life at the Fort

In the years after the French and Indian War, life at Fort Ticonderoga was hard. The British soldiers worked all the time. When they were not marching and drilling with their weapons, they had to work to keep the fort running. In the summer, some soldiers farmed the gardens just outside the fort walls. Other soldiers traveled by boat to get supplies from Canada. Winter work included chopping firewood to keep the troops warm. Also the soldiers replaced rotten pieces of wood and broken stones in the walls.

A few women spent winters at the fort to provide valuable assistance, such as help for the sick. Often the fort did not have enough food and supplies, so the men were hungry and ill. Many died from disease and hard conditions. The fort was not a pleasant place to live.

Defending the Fort

During the French and Indian War and later the **Revolutionary War**, if an army wanted to attack Fort Ticonderoga, it would have to attack from the land. The fort's position high on a rocky ridge made attacks from the water almost impossible. The shape of the fort helped in its land **defense**. The British soldiers could stand on the bastions to fire **muskets** and cannons at troops attacking the walls. Ditches outside the fort also protected the soldiers against enemy gunfire. The fort's soldiers fired artillery pieces on enemy soldiers and distant ships on Lake Champlain. They shot cannons, **howitzers**, and **mortars** to force back the enemy in different ways. The enemy army used the same types of weapons to attack the fort. Supply lines to other forts and to Canada were needed to keep the British fort going. Its soldiers would have to leave if they ran out of food and ammunition.

Fort Ticonderoga's iron cannons were aimed at the lakes to defend against attack by ship. The fort was the last line of defense during an enemy attack. The fort's commander held off an attack only until he could secure terms for giving up or until his soldiers could escape.

"The strength of the
Fort exceeds imagination."
-Eli Forbush, 1759
Massachusetts soldier

On May 10, 1775, American rebels surprised the British commander of Fort Ticonderoga. American patriot Ethan Allen climbed the steps to the commander's bedroom and shouted, "Come on out, you old rat!"

The Colonies Rebel

The British held Fort Ticonderoga after winning the French and Indian War in 1763. The American colonies **rebelled** against Great Britain in 1775. King George III sent British troops to stop the American Revolution. Before sunrise on May 10, 1775, Benedict Arnold, Ethan Allen, and the Green Mountain Boys, troops from nearby Vermont, quietly entered the fort and captured the British soldiers while they were sleeping. The British surrendered. This was the young nation's first victory of the Revolution.

During the winter of 1775–76, American colonel Henry Knox and his men transported 59 artillery pieces from the fort to Boston to help General George Washington's army. Then, in 1777, the British, under General John Burgoyne, recaptured Fort Ticonderoga by surrounding it with a large army. Later that same year, American general Horatio Gates forced Burgoyne and his troops to leave the fort and go back to Canada after the Second Battle of Saratoga.

Saving the Fort

After the Revolutionary War, Fort Ticonderoga was not used and began to fall down. In 1820, William Ferris Pell bought the old fort from two New York colleges that had been given the land. Pell built a large house and planted a beautiful garden on the grounds of the fort. Sixty-eight years later, Pell's great-grandson, Stephen Pell, and Stephen's cousin, Howland, climbed on the **ruins** of old Fort Ticonderoga. Stephen found a **tinderbox** from the days long ago when soldiers had lived there. This find started an interest in the old fort that lasted for the rest of Stephen's life.

When Stephen grew up, he married Sarah Thompson. He and Sarah began to have the fort repaired in 1908. President

Top right: *This flag from Fort Ticonderoga is one of the earliest existing American national flags.*
Bottom: *The Fife and Drum Corps marches in the Place of Arms, which is located in the center of Fort Ticonderoga. Reenactors often put on demonstrations about eighteenth-century military life for visitors of the fort.*

William H. Taft and other important people attended the opening of Fort Ticonderoga in 1909, which was 300 years after Samuel de Champlain had come to Cheonderoga with the Native Americans. Repair work on Fort Ticonderoga continued for many years.

Timeline

Native Americans use the Ticonderoga Peninsula for more than 10,000 years for camps and farms.

1609 - Samuel de Champlain and Hurons fight a band of Iroquois on the Ticonderoga Peninsula.

1755 - The French begin to build Fort Carillon on the Ticonderoga Peninsula.

1758 - On July 8, the French under Marquis de Montcalm defeat the British when the British attack Fort Carillon.

1759 - The French abandon Fort Carillon. The British repair the fort and rename it Fort Ticonderoga.

1775 - On May 10, Ethan Allen and the Green Mountain Boys capture Fort Ticonderoga.

1777 - On July 6, the British force the Americans to leave Fort Ticonderoga. In November, the British leave the fort after the Second Battle of Saratoga.

1783 - Fort Ticonderoga is visited by General George Washington and New York Governor George Clinton.

1820 - William Ferris Pell buys the old fort.

1908 - Stephen and Sarah Pell start the repair of Fort Ticonderoga.

1909 - President William Howard Taft attends the opening ceremony for the repaired fort.

"Key to the Continent"

The Ticonderoga Peninsula was called the "Key to the Continent" because it lay between the Champlain and Hudson valleys on the main trade route from Canada to America. The fort was attacked six times in two wars. On three occasions, enemy troops did not get past the outer defenses of the fort. Twice, defenders in the fort retreated when they were greatly outnumbered, and they used the waterway to escape.

This picture of Samuel de Champlain battling the Iroquois is from Champlain's own book about his life and travels. The fight took place on the Ticonderoga Peninsula on July 30, 1609. The battle was the first use of rifles in the Champlain Valley.

Fort Ticonderoga Today

Today Fort Ticonderoga is a fascinating place to visit. The old fort once again stands near the shores of Lake Champlain. Muskets, **powder horns**, the small tinderbox found by young Stephen Pell, and other objects are on display in a museum housed in the old stone barracks.

The Fife and Drum Corps performs music and artillery demonstrations daily in the summer. Special reenactments take place throughout the summer and fall. The King's Garden is a beautiful spot in which to learn about the time the Pell family lived near the ruins of the fort. Other sites to visit nearby are Mount Independence, Mount Defiance, and the French Lines on the Heights of Carillon where other battles in the French and Indian War and the Revolutionary War were fought. The 1700s come alive for visitors today at old Fort Ticonderoga.

Glossary

abatis (A-buh-teez) Piles of brush and trees sharpened and laid with their points outward in front of the walls of a fort.

allies (A-lyz) Groups of people that agree to help another group of people.

ammunition (am-yuh-NIH-shun) Bullets, shells, gunpowder, shot, and bombs.

artillery (ar-TIH-lur-ee) Large guns too heavy to carry, such as cannons.

barracks (BARE-iks) A building or set of buildings where soldiers live.

bastions (BAS-chunz) Works of earth, brick, or stone that stand out from a fortified work.

cistern (SIS-turn) A tank in which rainwater is collected and stored.

defense (dih-FENCE) To protect from attack or harm.

explorer (ik-SPLOR-ur) A person who travels to different places to learn more about them.

howitzers (HOW-it-sers) Short cannons that fire shells a short distance.

mortars (MOR-turz) Very short cannons that fire shells in a high arc. They are used to fire over fort walls.

muskets (MUS-kets) Long-barreled firearms carried by soldiers.

peninsula (peh-NIN-seh-lah) A piece of land that sticks out into water from a larger body of land.

powder horns (POW-dur HORNS) Containers for gunpowder that are shaped from the horns of cows.

powder magazine (POW-dur MAH-guh-zeen) A bomb-proof room for storing gunpowder and explosives.

rebelled (ruh-BELD) To have disobeyed the people or country in charge.

Revolutionary War (reh-vuh-LOO-shuh-nayr-ee WOR) The war between American colonists fought from 1775 to 1783 to win independence from England.

ruins (ROO-enz) Something that is damaged badly.

tinderbox (TIN der boks) A small box for holding flint, steel, and dry material for starting fires.

Index

A
Allen, Ethan, 17
American Revolution, 17
Amherst, Jeffery, 10

C
Canada, 6, 13, 14, 17, 21
Champlain, Samuel de, 5, 19
Cheonderoga, 5–7, 11, 19

F
Fort Carillon, 6, 7, 10
France, 6, 10
French and Indian War, 10, 13, 14, 17, 22

G
Great Britain, 6, 10, 17
Great War Path, The, 5, 6

H
Heights of Carillon, 10, 22
Hudson River, 5

I
Iroquois, 5, 11

L
Lake Champlain, 5, 6, 14, 22
Lake George, 5, 6

M
Marquis de Montcalm, 10

N
Native American(s), 5, 6, 10, 19
New York, 5, 6

P
Pell, Stephen, 18, 22
Pell, William Ferris, 18

R
Revolutionary War, 14, 18, 22

Web Sites

To learn more about Fort Ticonderoga, check out these Web sites:
www.fort-ticonderoga.org
www.historiclakes.org/Ticonderoga/Ticonderoga.html
www.digitalhistory.org/bfort.html